MW01623072

The Law of Attraction According To Jesus

ISBN: 978-1-09838-027-4

The LAW of ATTRACTION ACCORDING TO JESUS

Jim Kibler

CONTENTS

ACKNOWLEDGEMENTS

Mary Kibler, my wife and ministry partner, for her suggestions, editing and support.

Our Wonderful Church Family, for their support and encouragement.

Our Partners, whom I pray with every day.

All of God's people, who know that nothing is more important than being born again.

If you have never received Jesus as your Savior, just pray this prayer and you will be saved.

> **Heavenly Father, I repent for all of my sins. I believe Jesus is the Son of God and He rose from the dead after suffering for my sins. Lord Jesus, please come into my heart and be my Savior and I will serve You for all of eternity.**

If you just prayed this prayer and meant it with all your heart, you will spend eternity in Heaven with Jesus.

All Scriptural quotations are either from the King James Version, or Paraphrased.

DEDICATION

This book is dedicated to the memory of Eddie Jean Johnson, who went to join her husband and be with Jesus on July 19, 2020.

She was the Mother of our church, and editor of our books. This is the first book we have done without her and we miss her very much.

INTRODUCTION

If you are already practicing The Law of Attraction and getting everything, you want and you're happy with your life and what you're doing seems to be working for you, give this book to someone else.

But, if like many, what you are doing is not working for you, if you've read books by Law of Attraction experts, or taken classes with Law of Attraction teachers, or attended a Law of Attraction church, or you've coached with Law of Attraction coaches and you're disappointed, or frustrated by your lack of results, keep reading, your life is going to get much better.

The Law of Attraction According to Jesus is a true spiritual law and a true law works every single time, exactly the same way. When used properly, it will cause good things to happen for you and bring good things into your life. However, the truth of the matter is that millions of people are practicing what they think is The Law of Attraction and they are getting no results. If what you are doing is not working, it's time to do something different. This is different. This is The Law of Attraction According to Jesus and this Works!

The Law of Attraction According to Jesus has been working in my life for years. I know how to Attract good things into my life and into the lives of other people. I can Attract answers to prayer for myself and for other people. I can Attract healing into my life, or the lives of other people. I can Attract financial increase into my life, or the lives of other people. I can even Attract miracles. And I am not the only one who can Manifest these things. Some people you may have heard of can also do these things. There are people in my church doing some of these things, as well as some of my prayer partners around the world.

Jesus was the best example. He Attracted good things, wherever He went.

The Law of Attraction when used, "According to Jesus" will produce incredible results.

Some people just seem to Attract good things all the time. A coincidence? No. It is by design and you can do these things to. There is a simple way of causing yourself to Attract good things and we will discuss that in great detail in this book. There are also people who can make things happen and as your will see, that is part of the Law of Attraction.

Mark 9:23 All Things Are Possible to people who have faith. Let's start there. You have no impossibilities in your life. There is nothing you can't have, nowhere you can't go and nothing you cannot become. Now, you just need to know how to make these things happen. The Law of Attraction According to Jesus is your tool to Manifest all kinds of wonderful things in your life.

All good things come from God and we give God the credit for everything good that happens in our life. The objective of this book is to learn how to Attract God's Blessings, and all good things into our lives, to the point of Manifestation.

The Law of Attraction, according to New Age Believers, is the name given to the belief that "like attracts like" and that by focusing on positive, or negative thoughts, one can bring about positive, or negative changes in their life. That thoughts create spiritual power and energy and when focused properly, can cause good things to Manifest in a person's life.

The New Agers believe that the universe creates and provides for you according to what your thoughts are focused on. It is believed by many to be a universal law by which "Like always attracts like." That the results of positive thoughts are always positive consequences. The truth of the matter is that the universe is a creation, not a creator.

This same theory contents that Negative thoughts will create spiritual power and energy, which will Manifest bad or unpleasant things in a person's life.

The Law of Attraction, also known as "New Thought," is rooted in the belief that people and their thoughts, are made up of pure energy that Attracts other similar energies.

In the New Thought Philosophy, the Law of Attraction is a pseudoscience based on the belief that positive, or negative thoughts bring positive, or negative experiences into a person's life.

While this statement seems reasonable, the question must be asked, is there spiritual power behind positive and negative thoughts and is this spiritual power and energy strong enough to cause changes in a person's life. Can people effect changes, in their life, simply by changing their thoughts?

Unfortunately, The New Age Law of Attraction is based on theories.

The Law of Attraction According to Jesus, on the other hand, is based on God's Written Word.

There is no empirical scientific evidence supporting the New Age *Law of Attraction*. It is widely considered to be pseudoscience, which is a collection of beliefs, or practices mistakenly regarded as being based on scientific method. It is a theory set up to look for evidence, that supports its claims, but to this point in time has found none.

Supporters of the *Law of Attraction,* refer to scientific *theories* and use them as arguments in favor of it. However, it is considered not to have any scientific basis in the scientific community.

The New Age Believers subscribe to the theory that the mind is the most powerful tool you can use when it comes to Manifesting your desired reality. That everything you think about is going to reveal itself, at some point, in your life. They could not be more wrong.

Your Words are your most powerful tool, not your thoughts. Thoughts, which are unaccompanied by corresponding words, have no power, or energy, to create and Manifest anything, in the life of anyone. It is **Words** that have creative power and incredible energy, not thoughts. According to Jesus, what you say and believe, you will Attract and Manifest in your life, without fail.

That is why so many people who try the New Age Law of Attraction do not get any results. Read through some of the reviews that buyers of their books have posted.

You will see the phrase, **Attracting Words,** used frequently in this book. These are words, which will Attract either good or bad things into a person's life.

Positive people do tend to get more of what they want. Purveyors of Positive Thinking got this one right, at least up to a point. However, if your Law of Attraction teacher offers an explanation such as, your thoughts send out magnetic vibrations that literally Attract what you want to come to you, that is simply not true.

In this book when I use the term "The Law of Attraction" I am referring to The Law of Attraction According to Jesus.

There is, in reality, only one Real Law of Attraction and it is "According to Jesus" and it will always cause things to Manifest in your life. If you will practice The Law of Attraction According to Jesus it will change the course of your life and eventually bring you to a place of happiness, health, wealth, harmony and success.

CONTROL YOUR WORDS

This is absolutely the first step to achieving success with The Law of Attraction According to Jesus.

Thoughts are important, but According to Jesus and many other writers of the Bible, it is Your Words that Attract into, or Expel things out of, your life. You can actually learn to use your words to do either of these, any time you wish.

Words, not thoughts, are the most powerful force in the universe that control and shape the lives of human beings. Words, spoken in faith, will cause God to act on your behalf, or will allow the devil to do bad things in your life.

The Law of Attraction According to Jesus works, in the lives of everyone all the time, both positively and negatively. Considering the power of the words, that we speak **About Ourselves**; we must learn to discipline ourselves concerning our speech.

The words that we speak **About Ourselves** have creative energy and incredible power to Attract and cause Manifestation. Therefore, all words spoken in the future tense about yourself should be done very carefully and with purpose. Always be aware that anything you say About Yourself, in the future tense, will Attract what you say into your life.

The most powerful Manifestation tool is your voice.

Words, spoken in past, or present tense about yourself, will not Attract anything. It is only words, spoken in the future tense about yourself, that are what I call Attracting words.

People Have Ability To Create

This Biblical truth is rooted back as far as the beginning, when God said in **Genesis 1:26 Let us make people in Our Image, after Our Likeness and give them dominion over all the earth and everything in it.**

In our image, means that we are spirit body beings just like God. Our spirit however, lives in an earth body that God made out of dirt.

After Our Likeness, means that people are created to operate like God operates. God is a creating being, whose ability to create has no limitations and no bounds.

God creates with his Words, not His thoughts. He did not think about light and then see it. He **SAID**, “Let there be Light” and **then** He saw light.

We are creating beings. We create with our words also, but we have boundaries. Those boundaries are limited to our life and surrounding area in our ability to create.

Faith Filled Words

Newton’s law of motion states that Nothing will change its motion unless acted upon by an external force. The external force that will change our lives is our faith filled words. God’s law of motion, concerning our lives, might well be that a person’s life will continue on the same course, unless changed by **words** spoken in faith.

Faith filled words are words, spoken by a person, who actually believes what they are saying without any doubt. They also believe that what they are saying is true and will happen.

Words spoken, that are not spoken in faith, have absolutely no power or creative energy whatsoever.

Words spoken in faith, will go out into the spiritual realm as creative power and energy that will cause God to make changes in the life of the speaker. Faith filled words, both positive and negative, can affect a person's life, or the lives of their descendants, for years.

If you say something **About Yourself** and do not believe it, The Law of Attraction does not work. You must believe what you say, without a doubt, in order for your words to Attract, or Expel anything. The secret is getting yourself to the point where you actually believe what you say. In this book you are going to learn to do that and to reach the Manifestation point by using The Law of Attraction According to Jesus.

God's Law of Words

What would you think if God appeared to you and said, "From now on, everything you say **About Yourself** will come to pass?" That is exactly what God did say in Mark 11:23. Because of this, I would think you should be much more careful about what you say about yourself.

Actually, The Law of Attraction According to Jesus is based on this scripture.

> **Mark 11:23 For truly I say unto you, that whosoever shall say unto this mountain, (Obstacle, Blessing Block, or Problem) be removed, and be cast into the sea; and shall not doubt in his heart but shall believe that those things which he says shall come to pass; they shall have whatsoever they said.**

The simple explanation of this verse is that if you speak to a hinderance, obstacle, or Manifestation Block and tell it to leave your life, it will be Expelled, but **only if** you believe what you are saying, without any doubt. And if you say something, concerning your own life, or something within your area of authority, **either good or bad** and believe it, you will Attract it.

I don't think it was a coincidence that Jesus taught us how to Expel things, that Block our Blessings, and Attract Blessings in the same verse.

When you speak to spiritual blocks, like curses, or evil spirits, such as spirits of sickness and poverty, you must use the Name of Jesus in faith, to obtain results.

Action and Reaction

Newton's third law is: For **every action, there is an equal and opposite reaction**. This statement means that in **every** interaction, **there** is a pair of forces acting on the two interacting objects. The size of the forces on the first object **equals** the size of the force on the second object.

The amount of spiritual force used to Attract something good is the same amount of spiritual force needed to Expel, or push out something that is bad.

The second law of physics states that two objects cannot occupy the same space at the same time.

Manifestation Blocks

The Law of Attraction works the same way. When you are attempting to Attract something that you desire, into an area of your life, it is quite possibly pushing against an obstacle, or what I call a Manifestation block, that is in that same area.

Manifestation blocks, blockers, or what some people call abundance blocks, are roadblocks that will hinder you from experiencing Manifestation when using the Law of Attraction. Until you identify and remove these blocks you will have little success achieving your desires and the end result will most likely be disappointment and frustration.

> **Matthew 16:19 I give you the keys of the Kingdom of Heaven. What you bind, and prohibited from earth will be bound and prohibited from Heaven. What you lose, or allow from earth will be loosed and allowed from Heaven.**

When you bind, or prohibit a Manifestation Block, from your life here on earth, in the Name of Jesus, it is bound, prohibited, or expelled, by the Power of God, from Heaven. When you lose, or allow something, either good, or bad with your words, into your life, from earth, it will be loosed and Manifested into your life, by the power of God from Heaven.

It is much easier to Attract something good into an area of your life, after the blocks have been removed, instead of trying to Attract something, while there are blocks still in place. Unfortunately, this is what most people keep trying to do. Sometimes, there are several Manifestation blocks that need to be identified and removed.

For something good to come into your life, or to be Attracted, to the point of Manifestation, the Manifestation block must be removed, or Expelled.

Faith activates God's Power, or Spiritual Force, to Attract or Expel. The stronger your faith, the more Spiritual Power you have to work with and the faster you get to the Manifestation point.

While on this earth, Jesus had unlimited Spiritual Power because He was anointed with The Holy Ghost and with Power and His faith was perfect.

In Luke chapter 13, There was a woman in the Temple who was bent over and could not stand up straight. Jesus first cast out the spirit of infirmity, which was blocking her healing. Then by touching her, He Attracted healing to her body, which is something very good.

In **Mark 4:39 Jesus rebuked the wind and told the sea to be still.** Jesus first commanded the storm, which was causing the sea to be turbulent, to stop. Then, He commanded the sea to be still.

You cannot be sick and healthy at the same time, nor rich and poor at the same time. Cast out, or Expel, in The Name of Jesus, the block, which in many cases is an evil spirit. Then use your words and The Name of Jesus to Attract the good.

The way we Expel bad or evil spirits is by commanding them to leave in the Name of Jesus.

> **Philippians 4:10 At the Name of Jesus every evil spirit and curse will obey.**

This means every evil spirit of sickness and poverty.

When you tell something evil, or bad to leave your life, in The Name of Jesus, and believe that it will happen, with no doubt, it has to go.

Unforgiveness

> **Hebrews 12:15 Lest any root of bitterness springing up cause you trouble. This is how many people are defiled.**

A huge Manifestation Block, for many people, is unforgiveness and the root of bitterness. Go back in your life and if you are holding anything against anyone, ask God to help you forgive them. Every time you think about the person who offended, or cheated you in any way, or abused you in any way, speak a blessing over them. Just say "I Bless that person in the Name of Jesus and Lord, I ask you to let them have a good and happy day today." This will not affect them, but it will set you free and make it much easier for God's Blessings to Manifest in your life.

About Yourself

Whatever you say **About Yourself** will come true, or be Attracted to you, if you actually believe what you are saying.

This law applies to people speaking both positive and negative words **About Themselves**. It also applies to people who believe what is in the Bible and people who don't. In other words, it applies to **EVERYBODY!**

If you put out positive, Attracting Words, you will get positive results. However, it seems to be more difficult to believe positive statements **About Yourself,** than negative statements, because people have been conditioned to speak and believe negatively about themselves thinking this is being humble. Unfortunately, negative statements create Manifestation blocks.

The Bible refers to people who control their speech as being mature. Therefore, people who do not have control of their words are immature, which means not fully developed. That was me for a long time.

Words Can Be A Tool

So many people will say the first thing that comes to their mind without regard for the significance of what they are saying. They are ignorant of the fact that their words are constantly Attracting things into, or Expelling things out of their lives. The secret is how to use words, as a tool, to Attract good things and Expel bad things.

A wise person will weigh the consequences of what they are saying in any particular situation, because words matter.

The most important words however, are the words that we say, concerning **Ourselves.**

> **Hebrews 11:3 Through faith, we understand that God framed the worlds by His words.**

God also created us with the creating ability to frame our world, with our words, and make no mistake about it, your words do frame your world. God will also never override the words that you speak **About Yourself**. God is not in control of your life, nor the final authority as to what happens in your life, you are.

In Luke 1:20 The Angel, Gabriel, closed the mouth of Zacharias so he could not speak doubt and unbelief and override, or Expel the plans of God for the birth of John the Baptist through his wife Elizabeth. Your words have the power to override the plans of God for your life.

The Bible tells us in James Chapter 3 that our tongue is like the rudder on a ship that the Captain uses to turn the ship around. Or, like a small bit in the mouth of a horse, that can easily turn the large animal around.

If you practice the simple principles, outlined in this book, you will get to the point of actually using your words to Attract specific events, things, or changes, to happen in your life. Not as difficult as you might think.

Your life, over a period of time, will conform to the faith filled words that you speak **About Yourself** on a continual basis. This is true of everyone. No exceptions! The REAL SECRET is to make sure that you speak only positive words about yourself and eliminate the negative words, so as to Attract only good things.

Changing the words that you say about yourself, from negative to positive, is a process, but over time will result in Attracting the kind of life you have only dreamed about.

Control Your Life

If you can control your tongue, your words will Attract whatever you desire into your life. Do not be deceived by how simple this is.

Words in the Spiritual Realm

When you speak faith filled words, **About Yourself**, either positive or negative, those words go out into the spiritual realm and Attract things, or Expel things for years. They can affect your family, and generations who follow, for hundreds of years or longer.

You can use faith filled words, that you speak **About Yourself,** to Attract anything you need, or desire into your life. The trick is to change ordinary words into faith filled Attracting words.

Mary and I once had a great need for something and we did not seem to be getting any closer to getting it. We were talking about it one day and all of a sudden I said, "You know, I spoke months ago that we would have that. Those words are still out there and they will bring it to us. She said, "That's right." The next day we got it. I had changed ordinary words, that I had spoken months before, into faith filled attracting words and they very quickly caused what we needed to Manifest in our life.

Words spoken **About Yourself**, either positive or negative, if they are, or if they become, faith filled attracting words, will accomplish their purpose every single time. The Law of Attraction According to Jesus is a spiritual law and it works every time without fail.

Refuse to Accept Failure

Another secret is to refuse to accept defeat, failure, sickness, poverty, or lack of any good thing in your life. What you are willing to accept in your life will never go away. People stay sick because they accept sickness. People stay broke because they believe that is the way it's meant to be for them. Do not fall into this trap. You are meant to live an abundant healthy life. Don't settle for anything less.

Your Words Work For You or Against You

This is so simple. Make your Words Attract what you want, instead of what you don't want, by changing the words you are speaking **About Yourself**. Your words can be your best friend, or worst enemy.

Decide what words you are going to speak in any given conversation, or situation. Everything will soon be under control and eventually you will only Attract good things.

Negative words Attract things faster than positive words because people tend to believe negative comments more than positive comments.

Agree With God's Word Concerning You

Luke 1:38 And Mary said, Behold the handmaid of the Lord; be it unto me according to thy word. And the angel departed from her.

Mary **agreed** with the Word of God, when she was told that she would give birth to The Baby Jesus, even though she had never been with a man. Say the same thing that Mary said, concerning God's promises that pertain to you. There is something in the Bible concerning every situation that might arise in your life.

Change What You Believe

Joshua 1:8 Do not stop speaking God's Word out of your mouth so that you can do everything that is in it and you will prosper and have success in all that you do.

You can only hear something a certain number of times before you begin to believe it. If you want to believe something, in your spirit, repeat it to yourself over and over again, for weeks, or months, if necessary. Eventually, you will believe it. Usually, you can change what you believe in 90 days or less.

Hebrews 10:23 Do not stop speaking what you believe, with no doubt, because God is faithful to do for you what He has promised.

Your ear is four inches from your mouth and you are the first one to hear what you say. By speaking God's Word, regarding your situation, you are feeding your spirit, through your ear, and it will eventually increase your faith until you are believing what you are saying. Then Attraction begins and Manifestation follows.

The most powerful **Attracting Words** are God's Words concerning your life, or situation. Find them, speak them out loud, over and over again until they become faith filled words and then watch what happens.

The Flaps on The Side of Your Head

Mark 4: Jesus said, be careful what you hear.

I would add, or **who** you are listening to.

Guard the flaps on the side of your head, (Your ears). The words that go into your ears continually, both positive and negative, will go down and begin to grow in your spirit. These words will eventually come out of your mouth and Attract things that will change your life. I absolutely do not allow people who talk negatively, to spend time with me. **Stop giving negative people access to your ears!** They might Attract and cause some very bad things to Manifest in your life. I protect my ears from negative people and their words.

If you feed your spirit, through your ears with positive words, **About Yourself,** when you don't need them, your spirit will feed your mouth and cause it to speak positive **Attracting Words**, when you do need them. When a situation then comes up, you will find yourself speaking positive words about it and everything will soon work out to your advantage.

Ears Are the Gateway to Your Spirit

The words that come out of your spirit are faith filled words and will Attract or Expel. Make sure your spirit is filled with positive words.

The people you listen to actually have access to your spirit through your ears and will eventually, by the words they speak, cause changes to your life. This not only works for the person talking to you but also works through recordings and music. The truth of the matter is, you will begin to talk like the people you listen to and Attract what they have into your own life. Stop listening to people who are sick and broke and do not have the kind of life, or things, you would like to have.

If you are listening to good successful people, they can have a very good effect on your life. You will begin to talk like them and Attract what they have into your own life. If they are bad, unsuccessful people, they can have a very bad effect on your life. Be very careful who you give access to your ears.

Decide who you want to be like and only listen to those people. I only listen to a certain group of people and I am becoming more like them every day because I am Attracting the same kind of success into my life. They are very anointed and successful. I want to Attract that. Who are you listening to? If you do not want to become like a certain person do not listen to them, or their recordings.

Your Spirit Can Overflow

Matthew 12:34 out of the abundance (Overflow) of the heart (Spirit) the mouth speaks.

The word abundance means overflow, or too much for your spirit to hold.

Your mouth is the overflow valve of your spirit or heart. It seems that the spirit of a person can only hold so many words, either good or bad, before they spill out of your mouth and Attract things into your life.

When you begin to listen to another person talk, either person to person, on the phone, or through recordings, you are giving them access to your spirit. Nothing happens for a while. Eventually, your spirit becomes saturated, or overloaded with what you are hearing and their words will begin to spill out of your mouth. That will soon cause you to start thinking like them, talking like them and Manifesting what they have in your life.

90 DAY TURN AROUND

What you continually say, you will eventually believe. Then, when you say it, you will Attract it to the point of Manifestation.

When you change the words that you are saying **About Yourself**, from negative to positive, the complete turnaround will usually take 90 days before you begin to Attract good things and Repel bad things.

Abraham changed his words, at the age of 100, from negative to positive. His wife was 90, at the time, and they had no faith for the baby that God had promised them. God changed his name from Abram to Abraham which means father of many. He was then forced to call himself father of many, which at the time he was not.

90 days later this resulted in his 90-year-old wife becoming pregnant because, when his words finally became faith filled, what God had promised Manifested. Can you imagine what you can Attract and Manifest if you change your words for 90 days?

Just because God says something about you, does not mean that it is going to Manifest. You must also say it yourself and believe it before you Attract it.

A 90 Day Process

If you say only positive things about yourself, your health, your finances, your life, your circumstances, and situations for 90 days, without saying anything negative, you will begin to Attract positive things. If you keep doing it for one year your life will change. If you, do it for three years you will be living in abundance. And, If you keep it up for five years, you will be living your life on a level you never imagined.

How My Life Turned Around

Mary and I struggled for years to pay our bills. We would have to use all the faith we had, just to make our rent payments at the end of each month. Finally, about 10 years ago, I got a revelation that the problem was me. I was speaking negative words concerning my finances.

I decided to see how long I could go without saying anything negative **About Myself**. I bought a calendar and the plan was to give myself a check mark for each day that I did not say anything bad **About Myself**. After several tries, I finally had a whole week of check marks. Then a whole month. Can you imagine going one whole month without speaking any negative words **About Yourself**? But nothing changed, we were still struggling to pay our bills at the end of the first month.

Then two months went by without any negative words about myself. Still broke.

Then three months and now I really had something going, but we were still struggling to pay our bills. Nevertheless, I decided to see how long I could keep this going.

However, the fourth month was much different. Extra money began to come in from different directions. At the end of four months, we had money left over and we have had money left over at the end of every month, since the 90 days. We have never struggled to pay our bills, since that time. Without even realizing what was happening to us, we started to Attract money and soon our bank account began to grow. All the stress left our life and has never returned. Now we Manifest money and good things on a level we never imagined.

The key to our finances was definitely eliminating negative words about ourselves. Our finances and our whole lives had turned around in only 90 Days.

GET YOUR WORDS UNDER CONTROL

Put yourself on the same program. Get a Calendar and before you go to bed, give yourself a check mark if you have not said anything negative about yourself all day. Negative thoughts do not count against you unless you speak them.

> **James 1:19 Wherefore, my beloved brethren, let every person be swift to hear, slow to speak, slow to become angry.**

The key to this program is simple. Before you say anything **About Yourself**, think about what you are saying. Weigh your words carefully and speak very slow **About Yourself**.

If you do not control your words, they will destroy you. If you do control your words, they will Attract good things and enrich every area of your life immeasurably.

If you eliminate negative words **About Yourself**, the only words that will come out of **Your** mouth, **About You,** are positive words.

The rule of thumb is this. If you speak positive words, you will Attract good and positive things. If you speak negative words, you will Attract bad and negative things.

This is a process. Do not get discouraged if at first you have a hard time with this. You can do it, Anyone can! It gets much easier as you go along and before you know it, watching your words will become second nature to you. You will even become aware of how negative other people talk.

God's Method of Changing Things

Genesis 17:4 God said to Abraham, as it is written, I have made thee a father of many nations, before him whom he believed, even God, who quickens the dead, and calls those things which be not as though they were.

The key to this program is saying that you have something over and over again, even if you don't have it, **until you believe it.** Then when you finally say it and believe it you will Manifest it without fail. If you are not Manifesting what you are saying, just keep saying it until you do.

Joel 3:10 Let the weak say I am strong.

Speaking the opposite of what you actually have is how to Attract the opposite of what you have into your life. Say it even if you do not believe it at first. This works every time, if you keep at it. Usually, you will begin to see Manifestation in 90 days, **or less**.

If you call things that are, the way they are, they will stay the way they are, or get worse. If you call things that are not as though they were, continually, they will eventually change.

God's method of changing things is to call things that be not as though they are until it happens. God looked into the dark and said, "Light Be." I tell people, "If you want something bad enough, call it as though it were 100 times a day for 90 days."

This of course depends on your determination factor. If you cannot pay your bills, or if you are sick, your determination factor should be high.

You can change any area of your life by changing your words regarding that area for 90 days.

Abraham Called Things That Were Not As Though They Were For 90 Days

I guarantee you that when Abraham started calling himself father of many people, he did not believe it. But after doing this for 90 days he believed what he was saying and his 90-year-old wife became pregnant. He called something that was not, as though it was. The Law of Attraction started to work as soon as his words became faith filled Attracting words. What can you say about yourself for 90 days?

Paid off House

Several years ago, we owed twice as much on a house as it was worth. We had financed it at the peak of the housing boom and then the bottom dropped out and the houses in our area were worth half as much.

One night after midnight, I went out into the street, pointed my finger at the house and said out loud, "In the Name of Jesus, I call you sold and it will not cost us any money." Every time I thought about it, I said, "Our house is sold." Finally, the answer to our problem Manifested because two years later the house sold and it did not cost us one penny.

Be Slow to Agree With Anyone

If someone says something and you agree with them, it is the same as you saying it about yourself and you will Attract what they are saying.

One time, before church I overheard two people talking in the children's area. One person said, "Well, it's just one thing after another." The other person replied, "It sure is." Soon they were both Attracting one bad thing after another.

A few years ago, our next-door neighbor and his wife, who were absolutely wonderful Christian people, were leaving their home, of 55 years, to move into an assisted living facility. They were both very sad about leaving.

He came over to say good bye and said to me, "Well Jim, this is going to happen to all of us." I did not reply. He said it again and again I did not reply. He looked at me directly and said it a third time. I looked back at him and as gently as I could, said, "You are a wonderful person and we love you both, but that is not going to happen to us."

He was offended and I felt very bad but if I had agreed with him, the same thing would have eventually happened to us. I was not going to Attract that to Mary and me, even at the expense of losing a friendship.

> **Proverbs 13:20 He that associates with wise people shall be wise: but a companion of fools shall be destroyed.**

This verse is very important because everyone will soon act like and talk like the people they hang out with. Stop Attracting what foolish people have. Why do you think your mother was always concerned about the people you had for friends? She was concerned that you would become like them.

The Word Cycle

Galatians 6:7 Do not be deceived; God is not mocked: everyone will reap exactly what they sow.

Mark 4:14 The sower sows the word.

When you speak words **About Yourself,** either positive, or negative they go into your ear and are sown, or planted down into your spirit and will soon begin to grow and Attract, or Repel things according to your faith filled words.

When you keep sowing these words, the words keep growing, and soon will begin to come out of your mouth, back into your ear, and down into your spirit again.

Each time the words cycle they become stronger until they start Attracting change your life. If you speak some positive words and some negative words, it's like weeds growing with the flowers. If you keep planting, both in your spirit, they will soon Attract both good and bad things and lead to confusion.

Pick Your Area

To start with, decide which area of your life you want to improve. Your personality, health, finances or anything else you desire. Direct positive words toward that area intensely for 90 days and The Law of Attraction According to Jesus will cause these things to Manifest.

I Can Help You "If"

I tell people who call my Prayer Line, "**If** you watch your words, I can help you get healed, or to receive THE BLESSING

OF GOD upon your life. **If** you don't watch your words, there is nothing I can do to help you."

Control Your Future

If you control your words and say only positive words, that are well chosen, you can Attract what you want, control your future and guide your life in the direction you want to go. **YOU CAN DO THIS! Start today.**

Step 1. Watch your words

Step 2. Break the Curse of the Law, or have it broken for you.

Step 3. Have The Blessing, found in Numbers 6:22-27, spoken over you, in faith, by your father, priest, pastor or rabbi.

Now, we are going to use The Law of Attraction According to Jesus to accelerate the Manifestations of The Blessing in your life

BLESSINGS OR CURSES

Fact: God does not pick out people to bless.

Fact: God does not curse his people.

James 3:10 Out of the same mouth comes blessing and cursing. My brethren, this should not be so.

Everything you say **About Yourself**, will either Attract Blessings to your life, or Attract curses upon your life. Make sure that Blessings are Manifesting and that you are not cursing yourself, as most people do on a daily basis.

Choose Life or Death

Deuteronomy 30:19 I call heaven and earth to record this day against you, that I have set before you, life and death, blessing and cursing: therefore, choose life, that both you and your descendants may live.

According to The Bible, life, or death and BLESSING and cursing are all choices. There are two aspects of this. The first choice is life if we accept the terms of God's Covenant, and the 2nd is spiritual death, which is separation from God, if we do not choose life. Also, according to the New Testament, we choose life if we accept Jesus as our Savior and Spiritual Death if we do not.

The second, is the fact that we can choose BLESSINGS and reject curses.

This verse also mentions descendants, which means that these choices are generational. The choice of words that you speak during this lifetime will affect your descendants for years to come. Be careful.

Power of The Tongue

Proverbs 18:21 Your tongue has the power of life and death over you and you will live by the words that come out of your mouth.

Your tongue has absolutely incredible power over your life and you will live by the words that you speak. By your words you will bind and loose. Matthew 16:19 and Attract and Repel. Mark 11:23. All of us can have life, if we control our tongue regarding ourselves, and death if we do not.

How Curses Get Started

Genesis 9:25 and Noah said to his son, cursed be Canaan; a servant of servants shall he be unto his brethren.

Curses do not just happen; they must be voice activated by someone in authority. Very few people realize that negative things we say today, to and about ourselves and our children, actually invite and Attract curses and can affect us, our children and our grandchildren for years. Are you inadvertently cursing your children? This is one way that generational curses get started.

A spoken word can Attract curses, which remain in the spiritual realm and will affect and control lives, situations and circumstances indefinitely.

Many people are living under curses that have been spoken over them, either by themselves, parents, or ancestors. This is a major reason for sickness, poverty and lack in families, and in the lives of people. These can easily be broken. If you do not know how to break these curses, call me because I help people with this every day.

Generational curses, or curses of any kind and evil spirits, that accompany them, are Manifestation blocks and will never leave a person's life on their own. They must be broken, or cast out by someone who has great faith in the Name of Jesus. Then and only then, can healing, abundance and all the promises of God be Attracted and Manifested.

How Blessings Get Started

Genesis 28:4 and give thee the Blessing of Abraham to you and your seed.

When The Blessing of Abraham comes upon a person, it will automatically Attract and Manifest wealth, the good life and all types of wonderful things. It will also Expel bad things, such as sickness, poverty and debt.

Words we speak now **ABOUT OURSELVES,** or our children, have the potential to Attract things in our families for years to come.

Read Genesis Chapters 27 and 28. This is the story of Jacob and how his father spoke a BLESSING over him. Afterwards he went to his uncle's house to live and work. His uncle cheated him, deceived him and lowered his wages 10 times. Jacob nevertheless, became rich and finally became the owner of almost all of his uncle's herds.

All parents should speak Blessings over their children every day and their children will Attract success. When my son was little, I always said to him, "You are a good boy and a smart boy." That is exactly how he was while growing up and how he turned out as an adult.

The words you speak now, Attract either BLESSINGS or curses and can affect your family for thousands of years to come. It has been 4,000 years since Isaac spoke THE BLESSING over Jacob in Genesis 28:4. This BLESSING still affects the lives of all Jewish people and all born again people, who receive it, including me.

The Pastor's BLESSING

Pastors are **commanded** by God, in **Numbers 6:22-27**, to speak The WORD FOR WORD BLESSING over the people in their church on a regular basis.

The Lord Bless You and Keep You.

The Lord make His Face shine upon you.

The Lord lift up His Countenance upon you and give you peace.

These are God's Words and He wants them spoken over His people, word for word.

This is an incredibility powerful force in your life because if it is spoken in faith by the Pastor, it will Attract, Activate and Manifest the Blessing of Abraham in your life. Is this Word for Word Blessing being spoken over you on a regular basis? If not, why not?

Bless Yourself

Every time you speak positive words **About Yourself** you are actually blessing yourself and those words will cause good things to be Attracted and eventually Manifested in your life, unless they are nullified.

What you speak you hear, and what you continually hear, you will eventually believe. According to Jesus, in Mark 11:23, if you say something and believe it, it will always be Manifested in your life.

I will say this again, you can only hear something, anything, **a certain number of times** until you start to believe it. I tell people who are trying to Attract good things" Say you have it, until you get it!!!

My Determination Factor

In November of 2012, I received a revelation that The Blessing of Abraham was my inheritance. I knew that it belonged to me. I wanted it and I was determined to have it. However, I just did not know how to get it to Manifest in my life.

I started a program of sowing God's Word for The Blessing into my heart.

I started saying "The Blessing of Abraham is my inheritance, now Lord, You bless me." I intended to say this100 times every day. I even had the people in our church saying it. I said this over and over again, all day long, every day. I estimate that I said it 300 to 500 times a day. I did this, day after day, week after week and month after month, for 8 months. I spoke this for 240 days X 300 times per day = 72,000 times, at least. I was determined to have The Blessing come upon me.

The Blessing Block

I was Attracting The Blessing, but I now know that the reason, The Blessing of the Lord was not Manifesting in my life, was because the Curse of The Law was blocking it.

In June of 2013 the Lord spoke to me in an audible voice and told me I needed to break the Curse of The Law to allow The Blessing of Abraham to come upon me.

Of course, I quickly did what God told me to do. The Blessing Block was now gone. In only five months, our debt of $295,000 went away, evaporated. We now live an abundant, debt free happy life with no stress. Thousands of other people have also received The Blessing, because of what The Lord taught me.

It took me eight months to connect in Faith and Manifest God's Blessing. You do not have to spend eight months doing what I did, because I now know how to quickly Attract God's Blessing and have it Manifest in the life of anyone.

First the curse of the law must be broken, then the Blessing of Abraham can be spoken. When people call me, the first thing I do is break the curse of the law, that is blocking their blessing, and then I speak God's Word for Word Blessing over them. **Works every time!**

Never say, "I must be cursed." Always say, "I am BLESSED.

Never say, "I'll be damned." Always say, I'll be BLESSED."

Never say, "My kid is stupid and will never amount to anything." Always say, "My children are smart and will be successful at everything they do."

Never say, "I can't." Always say, "I can."

Men, always say, "My wife is beautiful, smart and very talented."

Women, always say, "I have a wonderful husband and He is handsome, smart and successful and a Blessing."

MANIFESTING HEALING

Fact: God does not pick out people to heal.

Fact: It is always God's will for all of his people to be healed. Remember, Jesus healed them **ALL!**

You can actually use **The Law of Attraction** to Manifest healing of any sickness and disease, as your body will respond to positive words that you speak about it.

A huge factor in whether, or not a person lives a healthy life, is what they are Attracting concerning their health.

Mary and I knew a wonderful couple who were very wealthy but had no control of their words, especially concerning their health. One or the other or sometimes both, were sick almost all the time. One day the lady said to us, "My husband is better now so I guess it's my turn to get sick." They did not realize that their words were Attracting sickness into their lives. They took turns getting sick. Soon afterwards, the husband got sick again and this time he died.

A Healed Heart

A lady from our church, Jean, was diagnosed several years ago with congestive heart failure. She was given between one month and a year to live. She could not walk more than thirty feet without stopping to catch her breath.

I took Jean to the doctor and he told us that she had congestive heart failure and that her heart was working at less than 40%.

He also said that she would not get any better and that he was just trying to keep her out of the hospital. She was very discouraged and for that matter, so was I.

When we got home, she sat down on the couch and I went back to the office. All of a sudden I got up, came out, stood in front of her and said, "We are not going to go by what the doctor said. From now on, every day we are going to say your heart is strong and getting stronger every day." Then I said, "Your heart is strong and getting stronger every day." Jean said, "My heart is strong and getting stronger every day." We both were calling her weak heart strong. Joel 3:10

We said this every morning for three months (90 days) and nothing changed. However, sometime during the 4th month, Mary and I decided to take Muffy for a walk and Jean said, "I am coming with you." She walked all the way down to the end of the block, rested and walked back. I said to Mary, "She is getting better."

We went back to the doctor and he said, "I just don't understand this, congestive heart failure does not improve, but the walls of your heart have become thinner and your heart is pumping fine." Of course, we told him what we had done. She went back to work, lived a normal, very productive life and was a key part of this ministry until she went to be with The Lord.

We had used The Law of Attraction According to Jesus, for 90 days, to Manifest her healing. What the doctors had said was a terminal heart condition was healed by the Power of God, which was activated by The Law of Attraction.

The Law of Attraction According to Jesus, when used properly, will Attract the Healing Power of The Holy Spirit, which will cause healing to Manifest in your body.

Generational Curses of Sickness

Many times, at the root of sickness and disease is a generational curse that has been running in a family for years. Doctors call these diseases hereditary. The truth of the matter is that any disease that runs in families is a generational curse which, in all probabilities, had been spoken by someone years ago.

Generational curses of sickness can be Attracted as easily as someone saying, "My kids get sick all the time." or, "Everyone in my family has a bad heart." or, "Breast cancer runs in my family."

Examples of generational curses of sickness are:

Heart disease

Cancer

Arthritis

Diabetes

High Blood Pressure

And Many More

Be careful that you do not Attract a generational curse of sickness in your family.

Expel Sickness and Attract Healing.

Step 1. Absolutely refuse to accept any sickness in your body. You will not experience the Manifestation of healing as long as you accept sickness.

Step 2. To be healed by God, of any sickness or disease, you must break, or Expel all curses and especially generational curses of sickness, by the Power in The Name of Jesus, or have it done for you. Curses are continual permission for spirits of infirmity, (Or sickness) to operate in your body. When these curses are broken, the spirits that cause sickness lose their spiritual legal right to be in your body. Sickness starts in the spiritual realm and so does healing.

Step 3. The spirits of infirmity, which give life to sickness, diseases, tumors and infections, and blocks healing, must also be Expelled, or as some people say, Evicted, in the Name of Jesus.

Step 4. Declare, or have someone declare, that you "Be healed in the Name of Jesus."

Step 5. To Attract the Manifestation of your healing faster, say continually "I am healed by the Stripes of Jesus." You can also add what I call, demanding prayers. Pray, "Lord, by The Stripes of Jesus, I am healed, now You heal me. I am a covenant person, now You Heal me."

Demanding prayers are a wonderful method to Attract and speed up the Manifestation of healing and they work every time, if you are determined.

If your determination factor is high and you keep at it, complete healing will be Manifested every time. It is OK to get help with this if you need help.

It is also very important to make sure that you have no sin, or unforgiveness in your life, as these are healing blockers.

Luke 4:39 Jesus Rebuked, Expelled, or cast out the fever in Peter's Mother-in-Law and she was healed.

If you have a major disease that is hindering your life, break the generational curse, cast out, or have someone cast out the spirit of infirmity, and then say, "By the stripes of Jesus I am healed" 100 times a day for 90 days and watch what happens.

Say The Opposite

Joel 3:10 Let the weak say I am strong.

If there is anything wrong with you physically, say just the opposite continually. If at any time I do not feel good I will say, "I don't feel good but I am getting better." Words about your health, spoken in the present or the past will not Attract anything. Just be very careful because words spoken in future tense will Attract and Manifest what you say.

So many people will cause a health problem to get worse by constantly making statements like, my legs are getting weaker all the time, I can't eat this or that, my back hurts all the time, my eyes are getting worse, I don't sleep well, I have this, or that. You get the picture. The condition of these people will continue to get worse because that is what they are Attracting.

They did a large study several years ago and found that people who rated their health as poor were almost three times as likely to die during the seven years of the study than people who rated their health as excellent. What are you saying about your health?

Why so many People Get the Flu

How many times have you heard people say, "We get the flu every year when it comes around?" Those people will get the flu every year because they are Attracting the flu with their words. Start saying, "We never get the flu at our house."

How Your Brain Responds to Words

The human brain responds much faster to negative words than to positive words. The reason is because negative words are perceived by the brain as a threat to survival. Any threat to survival, perceived, or real, causes acute stress and the body is not able to function properly, or rest.

Positive words propel the motivational center of the brain and also help to build resilience when problems arise. They are also shown to significantly lower both physical and emotional stress by Attracting peace and happiness in your life.

The Major Cause of Dementia.

Be careful that you do not Attract dementia because once Manifested it will destroy your life. I guarantee you that 99% of the people with dementia **Attracted** it, by saying things like, "I can't remember things like I used to, I am getting so forgetful, I forget things all the time." Instead, if you forget something, say, "I will remember it because I never forget anything. My mind is quick and sharp and I am getting smarter every day." The wellbeing of your brain depends on how you use the Law of Attraction.

Never, ever, under any circumstances say, "I can't remember." That statement alone will Attract dementia.

Develop a Strong Spirit

Proverbs 18:14 The Spirit of a person will sustain their sickness but no one can bear up under a weak spirit.

Every time you speak positive words, **About Yourself**, your spirit gets stronger and a strong spirit will cause you to say positive things about your health. This will Attract health and sustain you through any health issues.

Negative words will weaken your spirit and a weak spirit will not help you at all during any adversity. If you want to really strengthen your spirit speak God's Word concerning your life.

A Simple Cure For Depression

Negative words produce negative thoughts, which lead to fear, stress, anxiety, worry, and finally depression. Every time you feel depressed, cast out the spirit of fear in The Name of Jesus and then force yourself to say positive things about your situation, even if you don't believe it. Do this until you have Expelled the depression and Attracted the spirit of joy. You may be surprised because it won't take long.

Never Use These Words

The strongest stress producing words are the words NO and CAN'T. When used with the word I in the same sentence, such as saying, "I can't" or "No I can't" you are conveying a message to the brain that something is impossible for you to accomplish. This Attracts stress and a sense of failure.

You should absolutely never use the word CAN'T when talking About Yourself, as this word will greatly diminish your capabilities because it Attracts failure. The rule of thumb is, when you say, "I can't," you can't. The opposite is also true. If you say, "I can," you Attract the ability to accomplish tasks. No matter how difficult the task at hand is, just keep saying, "I can do this" and I guarantee you will eventually do it.

We have Attracted miracle healings for thousands of people with the Power in The Name of Jesus and faith fill words. Over the years, we have gotten thousands of prayers answered for people.

People healed off of death beds, some no longer eating, or drinking water and several gasping for every breath.

People full of cancer and who have lost most of their weight and strength, healed.

People paralyzed after having strokes, totally healed.

3 blind people healed.

3 people that I know of, who had severely damaged hearts completely healed.

Aggressive brain tumors disappeared.

2 brain dead people completely healed.

Several pancreatic cancer patients totally healed.

Many headaches went away instantly.

Blown out knees totally healed, some within minutes.

2 women, in the middle of miscarriages, stopped bleeding and carried their babies to full term.

Diabetes healed.

Blood pressure restored to normal range, including mine.

Kidney stones, including mine, healed.

Aggressive prostate cancer, that spread into the bones, totally healed.

People losing their mental capacity, completely restored.

Mass healings, where many people in a large crowd are all healed at the same time.

Never say, “I get sick all the time.” Always say, “I never get sick.”

Never say, “I am weak.” Always say, “I am getting stronger every day”

Never say, I can’t get over this sickness.” Always Say “I am getting better every day.”

Never say, “I can’t remember things anymore.” Always say, ‘I never forget anything because my mind is quick and sharp.”

Never Say, “I am getting old.” Always say “I am getting younger every day.”

Never say, “My health is poor.” Always say, “My health is excellent.” No matter what the condition of your health happens to be.

Never say, “I am so dumb.” Always say, “I am smart and getting smarter every day.”

MANIFESTING SUCCESS

Fact: Successful people are much happier than unsuccessful people.

Fact: You can use your own words to Attract a successful life for yourself.

Fact: People have a need to see progress in their life.

Visualize yourself as a success.

Behave as if you are successful.

Celebrate the success of others.

Success begins with a mentality of success. Everyday say, "I am the best at what I do, my product is the best, my service is the best and people like me." Be happy where you are at, on the way to where you are going.

Success does not mean the same thing to everyone. To me, the definition of success is a person who is stress free and happy, who has more money than they need to live on, who like themselves, who is living the life they truly want and feel that they deserve. I would also add in my case, doing what I want to do, where I want to do it and with the people, I want to do it with, making progress and learning new things every day.

Proverbs 13:20 The person who walks with wise people will be wise but a companion of fools shall be destroyed.

Success requires having a mindset that strives for success. Successful people talk differently and think differently than unsuccessful people. Associate with them and you will begin to talk like them, think like them, act like them and be like them. If you associate with unsuccessful people, you will become like them. In today's vernacular, if you hang out with fools you will become a fool.

Associate With Successful People

When I would join a new sales company one of the first things I would look for is the top sales people and those are the people I would try to make friends with. In any organization, the top 20% do 80% of the business. Also 20% of the people own 80% of the wealth in almost all free countries. This is called the Pareto Principle (80/20 rule). Hang out with the top 20% and you will begin to talk like them, act like them and Attract what they have. Sooner than you think, what they have will Manifest in your life and you will become one of them.

Change Your Thinking

If you have been unsuccessful, the first step toward Manifesting success is to renew your mind, by changing what you are listening to. Also, change the way you perceive yourself and talk about yourself. You must begin to see yourself as being successful in every area of your life. This begins with changing your words. Start by saying, "I am successful, I am the best at what I do, I am happy and there is nothing I can't do." Within 90 days you will begin to Attract success.

The Difference

Over one million kids play high school football each year and I am sure that every one of them would love to someday play in the NFL. A lot of these kids are very talented but, sad to say, only about one in five hundred will ever make it to the NFL level. What is the difference, you ask?

Have you ever watched NFL players being interviewed? Every one of them believes in their heart that they are better than anyone else at what they do. They talk and act like they are God's gift to football. It takes this kind of mindset to be successful at the NFL level. They believe they are special and that they are supposed to be there, doing what they are doing. They are right on all accounts. I have never heard a NFL player say anything negative about himself. NFL football players Attract success by their attitudes and especially by what they say about themselves and their ability.

Adopt this same attitude. Quietly apply these same principles to your job or profession and watch what happens. You will quickly rise to the top.

As you regularly speak words of success about yourself, negative thoughts of doubt about yourself and your abilities will gradually fade, and your success will be Manifested.

McDonald's

The first McDonald's restaurant opened in 1948. They became very successful during the next 15 years. People began to take notice and soon more fast food restaurants began springing up all over the country. Other people started selling hamburgers the same way. Then chicken, roast beef, fish, pizza followed. A lot of people made a lot of money marketing food exactly the same way. Copy a successful formula for business and you will be successful.

Whatever business you want to go into, find successful people doing the same thing, copy their method of operation, learn to talk like them and soon you will Manifest the same kind of success that they have.

If it's not Broke, Don't Fix it.

Many people will make changes to a successful program and then cry when things change for the worse.

If it doesn't work, change it quickly.

I have known so many people who were in trouble in their businesses and keep doing the same thing until they went broke. Years ago, Mary and I took over a restaurant that had very little business. At first, we also had very few customers but we constantly made changes until we found the right concept and menu. We were also saying, "We have a great business." Soon we had Manifested a great business. The rule is, if what you are doing is not working, SAY SOMETHING DIFFERENT AND DO SOMETHING DIFFERENT!

Never say, "Nothing ever works out for me." Always say, "Everything works out for me.

Never say, "I hate my job." Always say, "I love my job."

Never say, "This job is hard." Always say, "This job is easy for me."

Never say, "This is a terrible company." Always say, "This company is blessed because I am here."

MANIFESTING MONEY

Fact: Wealth is a Blessing.

Fact: Poverty is a curse.

Fact; There is no such thing as Luck. You are either Blessed, or you are cursed.

Fact: There is no such thing as a Blessing in disguise.

Fact: God does not pick out people to Bless, financially.

Fact: No one with The Blessing of The Lord upon them, can stay broke.

Fact: Most stress is caused by a lack of money.

Proverbs 10:15 The rich person's wealth is their protection: the poverty of poor people is destruction.

Money is important because Poverty causes destruction. It tears apart families and causes unbelievable stress in the lives of wonderful people. Not having enough money to live on and pay your bills is a terrible thing as many of you very well know. We are going to use The Law of Attraction According to Jesus to turn your finances around and cause you to Attract abundance, instead of Repelling it.

Have you ever listened to how most poor people talk **About Themselves**? Many of them are constantly cursing themselves, concerning their finances. To put it simply, they are Attracting and Manifesting poverty.

How often have you heard someone say, I can't afford?" Or, have you ever used those three words? Those words are Money Manifestation Blockers.

One of the most frequent reasons many people fail, when attempting to Manifest abundance, is because of how they perceive money. Start looking at money as a good thing, a useful tool.

Most poor people have been conditioned to despise people who are well off. They refer to them as "The other half." I love rich people because they are the ones who provide the jobs. I have never been hired for a job by a poor person. The rule of thumb is, you will never become like the people you despise.

If you want to become prosperous, don't complain about prosperous people. Do what prosperous and successful people do. Start talking like them and you will Attract what they have.

It's Not About Money

Neither prosperity, or poverty is about money, it's about a mindset. If you took all the money away from all the rich people and gave it all to poor people, within one year, the rich people would be rich again and the poor people would be poor again.

Years ago, I knew a Jewish man who invested all of his money and all that he could borrow from family and friends in a nightclub. Within three months he was out of business and broke. He and his wife came over to visit soon after and I said, "John, I am so sorry, what are you going to do?" He replied, "It's just money, I'll get it back." He was not even concerned because he knew his success did not depend on money, or any one business venture.

Generational Curse of Poverty

There is a curse of poverty flowing through poor families, because almost all poor people come from poor families.

> **Deuteronomy 28:29 and you shalt grope at noon-day, as the blind gropes in darkness, and you shall not prosper in your ways: and you shall be only oppressed and spoiled forever, and no person shall be able to help you.**

The word **forever**, in this verse, means that this is a GENERATIONAL CURSE OF POVERTY. It is characterized by a chronic lack of sufficiency in all things, especially finances.

Money can be Attracted by people who are living under this curse, but it is a never-ending battle. This curse will cause you to Repel money, instead of Attract money and it will keep you broke.

The vast majority of professional athletes, including those who earned millions of dollars, are broke within two to five years after they are retired. The reason is because even though they earned huge sums of money, the curse of the law has never been broken.

The curse of the law will allow generational curses of poverty to operate in the life of people and it doesn't matter how much money they have earned. They will still end up broke.

> **2 Corinthians 8:9 For you know the grace of our Lord Jesus Christ, that although He was rich, yet for your sakes He became poor, that we through His poverty can become rich.**

Jesus redeemed us from poverty by becoming poor Himself when He was stripped of everything He owned and hung on a cross. Unfortunately, the CURSE OF POVERTY has gotten back into the lives of many people.

Poverty is never a BLESSING in disguise. God is never glorified by poverty and poverty is never the will of God for anyone.

> **John 10:10 Jesus said, "I have come so that people can have life and have it more abundantly."**

Abundance is always a Blessing and poverty is always a CURSE.

Poverty is having less than you need on a continuous basis.

The Curse of poverty causes destruction to finances, which leads to destruction of families and that is its primary intention.

THE BLESSING and THE CURSE are Opposites

> **Proverbs 10:22 The BLESSING OF THE LORD, it makes people rich and God adds no hard work, or toil with it.**

The Curse of The Law makes people poor and the devil adds hard work and toil to it.

Almost all poverty has been Attracted by Generational curses of poverty.

Some poverty is caused by bad financial decisions, but that type of poverty is almost always temporary.

If a poor person had poor parents and grandparents, there is a Generational curse of poverty involved. This will operate down through the generations of that family until it is removed. This explains why money does not solve the problem of poverty.

What does solve the problem of poverty is breaking the generational curse of poverty, which is the main money Manifestation blocker.

Curses of poverty will always give unclean spirits of poverty and spirits of lack a legal right to operate in the life of an affected person.

Families who cannot pay their bills experience an incredible amount of fear and stress in their lives.

According to Proverbs 31:7 Poverty is misery and according to Proverbs 28:22 poverty is a spirit.

Because of Malachi 3:8-9, I do not believe that The Curse of Poverty can be broken from the life of any person who does not tithe.

Poverty is oppression of the devil.

All oppression, including Generational Curses of Poverty, are subject to THE NAME OF JESUS and can be broken by someone who has GREAT FAITH in that Name.

When I received a revelation that I had a Generational Curse of Poverty operating in my life, I went outside on the street at midnight and said, "In the Name of Jesus I break this Generational Curse of Poverty that is on my life." Immediately, I could physically feel something like a wet blanket being pulled up and lifted off of me. I felt light and free of a weight I did not even know I had been carrying. A few months later, things began to change and now we live in abundance.

I have had many people tell me they experienced the same thing when I broke the Generational Curse of Poverty in their lives for the first time.

The first breakthrough came for me when I got my words under control. The major breakthrough came when, through the direction of The Lord, I broke the Curse of the Law in my life and had The Blessing spoken over me.

Step 1. Expel all financial manifestation blocks from your life, by Breaking the Curse of the Law and all Generational Curses of Poverty, or find someone who can do it for you.

Step 2. Command all accompanying spirits of poverty, failure and lack to leave your life in the Name of Jesus.

Step 3. Attract The Blessing by Having God's Word for Word Blessing, found in Numbers 6:22-27, spoken over you by your Pastor, Priest, Rabbi, or Teaching Minister, where you tithe, on a regular basis.

Once the Curse has been expelled it is very easy to Manifest the Blessing because there is nothing to block it. However, The Blessing will not come into your life as long as the Curse of the Law is in place. The only way to Expel the Curse of the law is with a command using The Name of Jesus, in faith.

This is the easy way to Attract money because the Blessing of The Lord will automatically remove your debt and cause abundance to Manifest in your life, over a period of time.

When people, who are broke, come into my church, or call me, I break every generational curse of poverty and the curse of the law in their lives. I then command every spirit of poverty to leave them. Lastly, I speak God's Word for Word Blessing over them and tell them to watch their words.

I tell people that they will usually see results in six months or so. In only five months we had $295,000 in debt evaporate and we had more than enough money to pay our bills. Soon after that we began to accumulate money.

Speed up the Manifestation

The Blessing of The Lord is going to cause abundance to come to you, but you can also speed it up by using the Law of Attraction According to Jesus.

Call things that be not as though they were until they are. Romans 4:17

Say this, word for word, 100 times every day. The more intense and determined you are the faster it works.

Money comes easy to me. I attract money. I am living in abundance. I have more than enough money. God provides all my needs, according to His riches in Glory, by Christ Jesus. My bills are paid and my debt is gone.

Attract The Power to Get Wealth

Deuteronomy 8:18 But you shall remember the Lord your God because it is He who gives you the power to get wealth to continue His covenant which He made with your fathers and it is still the same today.

The power to get wealth is a force, that comes from God, and it will cause you to Attract abundance on a level you never imagined. You will, actually, become a money magnet.

This is reserved for God's covenant people, which is all Jewish people and also non Jewish people who are born again Christians. If that is you, you can claim this Power for yourself by first casting out the spirit of poverty and then saying 100 times a day for 90 days, "Lord I am a covenant person, now You give me the power to get wealth. I know I have the covenant of wealth and the power to get wealth." Keep saying this until you believe you receive it and then, according to Jesus, it will Manifest in your life.

This is a process, but many times financial breakthrough comes very quickly. I have even seen huge financial Manifestations happen overnight. The faster you increase your faith, the faster you will increase.

A lady came to me after church one Sunday and said, "I lost my life savings in an investment that did not work out. I have no way of getting the money back as I am on a fixed income." I replied, "I don't know how God is going to do it but you are going to get that money back. As a matter of fact, you are going to get three or four times as much." She said, "Ok" and walked away. She did not mention it again, but one year later, she received an unexpected inheritance check for almost four times what she had lost. My words, spoken in faith over her had caused her to Attract that money and a year later it had Manifested.

A contractor told me he had built four commercial buildings that he was unable to sell and because of that he was going broke. I said, "I don't know how God is going to do it but your buildings will all sell quickly and at a good profit. And furthermore, God is going to give you a huge blessing on top of that." Within thirty days, all four building were sold and one year later he walked into a quick deal and made one million dollars for himself. My words over him caused huge blessings to Manifest in his life.

Things like this happen on a routine basis in my prayer ministry, because I speak Attracting Words over people. We have Manifested Financial Blessings for thousands of people and we get financial praise reports almost every day.

Never say, "Times are hard." Always say, "Times are always good for me."

Never say, "It's tough to make money these days." Always say, "Money comes easy to me."

Never say, "Everything I touch turns to garbage." Always say, Everything I touch turns to gold."

Never say, "I can't afford this." Always say "I can have anything I want."

Never say, I am broke." Always say, "I will never be broke, another day in my life."

Statements that Attract money:

I am a money magnet.

Money is good.

I am attracting more money each day.

I am ready to receive all the wealth I deserve.

There is no limit to how much money I can attract.

Wealth and Riches are in my house.

I will always have more money than I need."

"Earning money is easy for me.

"I live a successful, abundant, joyful life."

MANIFESTING YOUR DESIRES

Manifestation is the process of turning a specific desired outcome into a reality, through an intentional action.

Manifestation Step 1. Choose What You Want To Manifest

Ask Yourself: Do I really want this and how important is it in my life?

Manifestation Step 2. Expel, in The Name of Jesus, whatever it is that is occupying the area of your life that you want to change. These are Manifestation Blocks. Examples: If you desire to be loved, first remove any hate that might be in your life. If you desire to be healed, first remove the spirit of infirmity which is causing sickness. If you want your finances to increase, first remove the spirit of poverty.

Unfortunately, there will almost always be something blocking your way to success. This shouldn't scare you; this is just part of the whole manifestation process.

Manifestation Step 3. Stop living in the past: There is a sign on the door to my past that says: Pastor Jim doesn't live here anymore.

Manifestation Step 4. Stay away from Toxic people: When you are working on Manifesting your dreams, you need to make sure no one is holding you back.

Manifestation Step 5. Keep saying you already have what you want to Manifest.

This is God's law of calling things that be not as though they are until they are.

Don't think, or fuss about how or when your desired object or outcome will manifest and don't try to see it coming to you through any particular person, or means. God will decide how to get it to you. Your focus should be on the end result of receiving the thing of your desire.

Manifestation Step 6. Appreciate what you get and thank God for it. The more gratitude you show God, the more He wants to do for you.

Manifest Answers to Prayer

Mark 11:24 I tell you this, anything you desire, when you pray, expect to receive it and you will have it.

The key to answered prayer is to ask God for something, (Anything) and get yourself to the point where you expect to get it, and then it will Manifest in your life.

If you are praying to God for money to buy something, or to pay the rent, start thanking Him for it. Then say continually, "I have the money for whatever I need" until it Manifests, which it will.

Kenneth Hagin received his healing, years ago, simply by believing God's Word and saying, "I believe I receive my healing."

1 Samuel 1:17 Go in peace and The God of Israel give you what you have asked of Him.

A great way to quickly Manifest the answer to Prayer is to have someone, who has great faith, declare that God will give you what you desire, just like Eli did for Hanna.

How to Do A Personality Makeover

Everyone likes people who have good personalities. Speak positive words about everything and everyone. If people do not seem to like you, or want to be around you start saying, "I am a wonderful person and people like me." Do not be disagreeable. Make an effort to be pleasant and smile. You will be amazed by how fast people will begin to be Attracted to your new personality.

How to Be Happy

Happiness starts with a decision. Make a decision to be happy and start saying, "I am a happy person and people like me." Do this every day for 90 days. You will Manifest happiness in your life and people will like you.

Years ago, we made a decision to be happy, no matter what, and we have actually been happy ever since.

How to Quit Smoking

Most people fail when they try to stop smoking. The easy way to stop smoking is that every time you light up a cigarette just say out loud, "I do not desire to smoke." If you do this **every time** you light up, your desire to smoke will be **Expelled** and you will stop smoking in 90 days with no pills and no patches.

How to Lose Weight.

We all know that diets do not work. The truth of the matter is that if you take into your body less calories than you need, you will lose weight and if you take in more than you need, you will gain weight. The answer is, take in less.

The way to do this is simple. Every time you sit down to eat, before you take a bite say, "I do not desire to over eat." Do this for 90 days and the weight will begin to come off. The desire to overeat will be Expelled. A man in Arkansas did this and lost 120 pounds.

It also helps to say continually, "I do not desire to eat sweets and ice cream."

A Wonderful Husband

Ladies, if you are single and desire to have a husband, have the curse of bad relationships broken, if that is a problem. Then say, "I have the perfect husband for me" 100 times a day for 90 days and you will Attract a wonderful husband. Remember, Jesus said, "All things are possible for them who believe." After saying it for 90 days you should start believing that you have the perfect husband and you will receive the Manifestation. We have had this happen many times.

Increase Your Intelligence

Would you like to be smarter? You absolutely can.

I use to be a terrible speller but after 90 days of saying "I am smart and getting smarter every day I had Attracted an increase in my intelligence and I could spell just about any word.

I flunked high school chemistry because I just did not understand anything that was going on in that class. One evening,

I picked up my stepson's college chemistry book and spent the entire evening reading through it. I understood everything perfectly and if I took that college class today my grade would most definitely be an A. I really am getting smarter every day and so can you.

When I am working with a new software program, or platform, I always say, "I am smart and I will learn this." I always do.

Every semester, when my son was in college, I would speak over him and say, In the Name of Jesus, you have a supernatural knowledge of all the material you are learning this year." It worked! I also do that for the people in my church and my prayer partners on a regular basis.

How to Attract Good Looks

Ladies, look in the mirror every day and say "I am getting more beautiful every day." In 90 days, everyone else will agree with you and people will turn their heads to look at you. Men, every day say, "I am getting better looking every day." Everyone should say every day, "My youth is renewed like the eagles" Do this for 90 days and watch what happens. You will Manifest youth and beauty and people will notice.

How to Manifest Good Sleep

How many people have you heard say "I don't sleep well at night." Guess what? They will never sleep well at night if they keep talking like that. If you want a good night's sleep, just start saying, "I sleep good at night." Say this on a regular basis. You will Attract good sleep and very soon you will sleep like a baby.

Never say, "Tomorrow is going to be a hard day." Always say, "Tomorrow will be better than today"

Never say, I am such a loser." Always say, I am a winner at everything I do."

Never say, "I can't do anything right." Always say, I can do anything."

Never say, "I am so unhappy." Always say, "I am a happy person."

Always say, "I am a wonderful person, I have a great personality and I am happy all the time."

Always say, Pastor Jim is a wonderful Pastor and the best prayer partner in the whole country

MY LAW OF ATTRACTION QUOTES

1. Jesus said," You will get what you say and believe you have."
2. The Law of Attraction According to Jesus is always working in your life, whether you believe it or not.
3. To Attract anything into your life say "I have it" until you get it.
4. You have no impossibilities in your life.
5. What you say continually is what you will Attract and Manifest in your life.
6. The Law of Attraction According to Jesus Attracts things to you, according to your faith filled words.
7. Ask God for what you want and then say "I believe I receive it" until it has Manifested.
8. Keep your words fixed on what you desire to have in your life, not what you don't want.
9. Your words have creative power in your life.
10. Your words will Attract Blessings, or Attract curses to come upon you.

11. What you say, you create in your life.
12. You create your words and your words create for you.
13. The power to Attract change in your life lies in your words.
14. When you truly want something and keep saying you have it, you will eventually have it.
15. The words you speak will go into your ear, down into the soil of your spirit and produce a harvest that corresponds to what you said.
16. Every moment is an opportunity to change your life because at any minute you can change what you are saying about yourself. Mary says, "A minute may change the rest of your life."
17. If you are wondering what will be Attracted into your life tomorrow, remember what you said about yourself yesterday.
18. You can control your emotions with your words.
19. There is no shortage of what you want, or need. Just say I have it until it is Manifested.
20. If you continually say, "Everything works out for me" everything will soon begin to work out for you.
21. If you continually say, "The rest of my life is the best of my life" it will be.
22. What you say you are, you become.
23. What you say you have, you Attract.
24. If you are excited about something, it's because your spirit knows it is coming to you. Excitement is the Manifestation gage.

25. Focus your words on what you want.
26. Don't talk about what you don't want.
27. The secret to having it all, is saying and believing you already do.
28. If you want to be rich, think and talk like rich people.
29. You become what you say and believe.
30. Learn to trust that your words will bring God's Blessings to you, because they will.
31. You are today where your words have taken you. You will be tomorrow where your words take you.
32. No one has the choice of whether or not to live by their words, but you can decide which words you live by.
33. Say this every night, "Tomorrow will be better than today" and it will be.
34. Say, "I am a money magnet" and you will Attract money.
35. If you realized how powerful your words are, you would never say another negative word about yourself.
36. God does not make you wait, when you say I have something and actually expect it.
37. Negative thoughts are harmless unless spoken and then they can be very destructive.
38. Use these powerful positive words, I have, I am, I can.
39. Never use these powerful negative words. I can't, this is hard.
40. If you can keep saying it you will Attract it.
41. Whether you say you can, or say you can't, either way you are right.

42. Everything you want is out there waiting for you to Attract it into your life with your words.
43. When I say I can and believe I can, I Attract the ability to do it.
44. Take charge of your life, begin Attracting and Manifesting all that you desire in life with your words.
45. Your whole life is a Manifestation of the words that have come out of your mouth.
46. Change your words and you change your world.
47. Once you replace negative words with positive ones, you'll start receiving positive Manifestations
48. Say I am living in abundance, on a continuous basis and you will Attract abundance.
49. You can have, do, or be anything you say.
50. To achieve goals you've never achieved before; you need to start saying things about yourself, you've never said before.
51. Speaking negative words is the single greatest Manifestation block.
52. You can't change your future by looking at, or talking about your past.
53. You can use your words to shape your future into whatever you want it to be.
54. Say people love giving me nice things and you will Attract lots of nice things.
55. Positive thoughts do not Attract anything unless you speak them.

56. If you want to be successful, find a bandwagon full of successful people and jump on.

ABOUT THE AUTHOR

Pastor Jim Kibler was born in Pittsburgh and grew up in Slippery Rock, Pennsylvania. He is a graduate of Mount St. Mary's College in Emmitsburg, Maryland, and Rhema Bible College in Tulsa, Oklahoma. He also did graduate work in business at George Washington University in Washington, DC.

Pastor Jim and his wife Mary, who is also a graduate of Rhema Bible College, Pastor Life Church in Indialantic, Florida.

Pastor Jim's popular website is www.increasenow.com, a **FREE SITE**, where people around the world watch his FREE 15 Minute videos every day. He teaches about God's Goodness, Healing, Redemption, Abundance and The Blessing.

Also watch Pastor Jim's 15 minute videos every day.

Subscribe To Pastor Jim Kibler on YouTube

In addition, Pastor Jim is a Very Entertaining Conference Speaker and everywhere he speaks, people get healed, finances increase and churches grow. He makes God's Word very easy to understand. He also has a very anointed healing ministry with people being healed of every type of disease and blind eyes opened.

Pastor Jim has a wonderful Prayer Ministry and makes himself available to pray with people who do not have a Pastor to pray with them. He is Personal Pastor to many people who otherwise do not have a Pastor to Talk to, Speak THE BLESSING over them, or Pray the Prayer of Faith for their needs.

His Prayer Ministry has had incredible results. Many people are healed right over the phone, have the curse of the law and generational curses broken and have THE BLESSING activated in their lives.

Pastor Jim's phone number is available at www.increasenow.com

He is called the **"How To Preacher"** because he not only teaches people what God has promised, but how to receive it.

Other Books by Pastor Jim:

"The Blessing"

"Jesus"

"How To Pray"

"The Blessing and The Tithe

"The Power of Positive Words"

"Faith"

"How To Break Curses"

"How To Get A Miracle"

"If The Bible is True"

Made in the USA
Coppell, TX
20 July 2021